Review & Analysis of
Maxwell's Book

Everyone Communicates, Few Connect

BusinessNews Publishing

BOOK PRESENTATION: *EVERYONE COMMUNICATES, FEW CONNECT* BY JOHN C. MAXWELL

BOOK ABSTRACT

MAIN IDEA

You, like everyone else communicate all the time – whether you realize you're doing that or not. To become a genuinely effective leader, however, you have to learn how to connect with other people in everyday situations. Connecting this way requires that you first understand the five key principles of connection and then apply the corresponding five key practices:

You can always learn a lot by observing good leaders and communicators in action but your most intensive training will come as you work to apply what you observe. As you learn through trial and error what works and what does not, you can enhance your own ability to connect with others. The challenge in leadership is always to take what you have and to make the most of it rather than obsessing over what you don't have. Connecting with people will make that happen.

> *"If you want to learn how to connect and thereby become more effective in everything you do, there's good news. Even if connecting with others isn't something you're good at today, you can learn how to do it and become better tomorrow. Learning to connect with people can change your life."*
>
> *– John Maxwell*

ABOUT THE AUTHOR

JOHN MAXWELL is a leadership expert, speaker and author. He has written more than 50 books which have sold over 18 million copies worldwide. Three of his books have sold more than a million copies each: *The 21 Irrefutable Laws of Leadership, Developing the Leader Within You* and *The 21 Indispensable Qualities of a Leader.* Dr. Maxwell is a graduate of Ohio Christian University, Azusa Pacific University and Fuller Theological Seminary. He is the founder of EQUIP, a non-profit training organization which has trained in excess of 5 million leaders in 126 countries. John Maxwell speaks every year to a wide variety of organizations including Fortune 500 corporations, government leaders, the United Nations, the National Football League and the United States Military Academy at West Point.

Dr. Maxwell's Web site is at www.JohnMaxwell.com.

IMPORTANT NOTE ABOUT THIS EBOOK

This is a summary and not a critique or a review of the book. It does not offer judgment or opinion on the content of the book. This summary may not be organized chapter-wise but is an overview of the main ideas, viewpoints and arguments from the book as a whole. This means that the organization of this summary is not a representation of the book.

SUMMARY OF *EVERYONE COMMUNICATES, FEW CONNECT* (JOHN C. MAXWELL)

1. FIVE KEY PRINCIPLES OF CONNECTION

Connecting is purely and simply built on your ability to identify with people and relate to them. To become more productive and influential as a leader, you have to learn how to genuinely connect with others. To pull this off in real life, you have to understand five key principles about making personal connections:

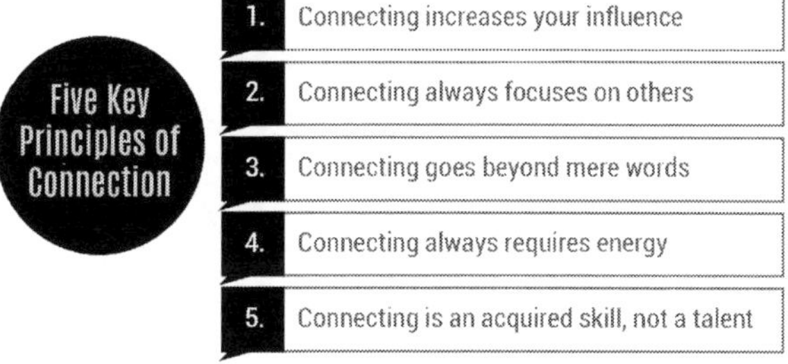

1. CONNECTING INCREASES YOUR INFLUENCE

People are always far more influenced by the depth and credibility of the connection you form with them than they ever are by the quality of your materials or even by the smoothness of your presentation. A genuine and sincere sense of connection can overcome all kinds of other difficulties and challenges.

In fact, one study of sixteen thousand executives (summarized below) suggested there is a direct and measurable correlation between achievement and the ability of an individual to connect with people. When you compare the characteristics of high, average and low achievers, it soon becomes clear communication abilities are a key differentiator.

> *"I am convinced more than ever that good communication and leadership are all about connecting. If you can connect with others at every level – one-on-one, in groups, and with an audience – your relationships are stronger, your sense of community improves, your ability to create teamwork increases, your influence increases, and your productivity skyrockets."*
>
> *– John Maxwell*

It's clear your ability to connect can make or break what you do in every area of your professional career and personal life. If you're good at connecting, you're going to achieve more. You position yourself to make the most of your own talents and abilities. This, in turn, means you will be more productive.

Although it may sound somewhat counterintuitive at first, the smaller the group you're working with, the more important it becomes to be able to connect. Great leaders are always highly competent at connecting with people one-on-one, in a group setting and when giving a formal presentation in front of an audience.

To become better at connecting:

- Get into the habit of talking more about the other person and less about yourself and your own interests.
- Always try and inject a useful thought or idea into every interaction you have.
- Find ways to compliment what other people are doing.
- Be on the lookout for ways to add value to a group.
- If you're fortunate enough to have some successes, acknowledge the role others have played in what was achieved.

> *"If I went back to college again, I'd concentrate on two areas: learning to write and to speak before an audience. Nothing in life is more important than the ability to communicate effectively."*
>
> *– Gerald Ford, 38th president of the United States*

> *"The number one criteria for advancement and promotion for professionals is an ability to communicate effectively."*
>
> *– Harvard Business Review*

"Those who build great companies understand that the ultimate throttle on growth for any great company is not markets, or technology, or competition, or products. It is the one thing above all others – the ability to get and keep enough of the right people."

– Jim Collins, author, Good to Great

High Achievers	Average Achievers	Low Achievers
↑ Worry just as much if not more about the people involved in the transaction at hand as they do about making a profit	↔ Concentrate first and foremost on production issues and don't pay much attention to the personalities involved	↓ Are so preoccupied worrying about their own security they never get around to thinking about their customers' needs
↑ View their subordinates optimistically and look for ways to get them involved	↔ Focus pretty much exclusively on their own status	↓ Show a basic distrust of subordinates and what they can contribute
↑ Are always willing to seek advice from those who report to them	↔ Are reluctant to seek advice frome those who report to them	↓ Tend not to seek advice from anyone
↑ Are prepared to listen to anyone and everyone who has a good idea	↔ Listen only their superiors	↓ Avoid most communication and rely instead on policy manuals

2. CONNECTING ALWAYS FOCUSES ON OTHERS

When you're trying to connect with someone else, keep in mind it's never about you – it's always about the interests and preferences of the person you're interacting with. Focus on what's important to them and you will be one of the most interesting people they've ever met.

This may sound obvious but there are all kinds of reasons why people can forget to focus on others:

- Maturity issues may cloud your judgement and encourage you to be self-centered rather than outward looking.

- You may have an overdeveloped ego and an unrealistic sense of self-importance.
- You may be so focused on your own agenda you don't give the input of others a reasonable weighting.
- You may be trying to do everything yourself rather than harnessing the input of others to maximum effect.
- You may lack confidence and feel insecure.

To offset and overcome these kinds of issues and make genuine connections, you have to keep in mind whatever you do has to answer the three basic questions everyone asks:

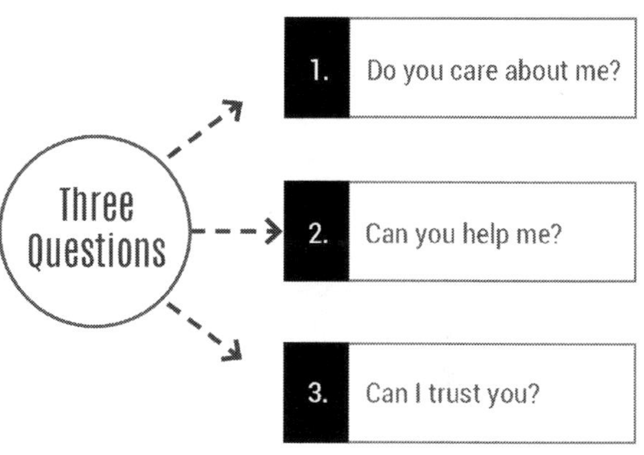

1. *Do you care about me?* If you feel the person you're interacting with genuinely wants to help, then you're more likely to feel connected. Similarly, to form worthwhile connections and influence other people, view them as individuals you'd like to associate with and spend time with rather than merely as numbers in your monthly quota.
2. *Can you help me?* We always connect with people who can do good things for us. It's just a natural instinct. With this in mind, if you can demonstrate beyond any doubt you will add value to an interaction, you will connect. Or put another way, when you talk with people, focus on benefits – what your product or service does for them – rather than features. In an information saturated world, you get people's attention when you show you can and will help them.
3. *Can I trust you?* Again, we form deeper connections with someone we trust than we ever do with those who are working to their own agendas. To make more connections, you have to be unquestionably and totally trustworthy.

Overall, if you can get into the habit of thinking about the other person's perspective and then exploring what's important to them, you will always connect.

> *"You can connect with others if you're willing to get off your own agenda, to think about others, and to try to understand who they are and what they want. If you really want to help people, connecting becomes more*

natural and less mechanical. It goes from being something that you merely do to becoming part of who you really are. If you're willing to learn how to connect, you will be amazed at the doors that will open to you and the people you will be able to work with. All you have to do is keep reminding yourself that connecting is all about others."

– John Maxwell

"If you will first help people get what they want, they will help you get what you want."

– Zig Ziglar

"We aren't in the coffee business, serving people. We're in the people business, serving coffee."

– Nabi Saleh, owner, Gloria Jean's Coffees

"If you would win a man to your cause, first convince him that you are his sincere friend."

– Abraham Lincoln, 16th president of the United States

"Some singers want the audience to love them. I love the audience."

– Luciano Pavarotti, Italian opera tenor

"I get a speech over with because I love people and want to help them."

– Norman Vincent Peale, pastor and author

3. CONNECTING GOES BEYOND MERE WORDS

Whenever you try and connect with someone, you may at first assume what you say is the deciding factor in whether or not you connect. This is incorrect. To make a genuine connection, you have to connect at four different levels:

1. Visual
2. Intellectual
3. Emotional
4. Verbal

- *Visual* – the other party has to see you're paying attention to them rather than attempting to do several things at once. Often, this is a matter of eliminating distractions. If you're talking on a cellphone, then it's unlikely the other person will be motivated to tell you their most heartfelt issues. Similarly, if you're poorly groomed or wearing completely inappropriate clothing, you're not exactly laying a good foundation for becoming influential. After you address these basics, you also have to learn how to be outwardly expressive. If you always talk with a poker face, people will feel uneasy around you. You have to signal with your facial expressions that you are enjoying the conversation. Smile a lot. Move around with a clear sense of purpose. Have an open posture. Try and get rid of any barriers between yourself and the person or people you're trying to communicate with. Take full responsibility to continually give others the verbal clues you're present and engaged in what they're saying rather than distracted and uninterested. Make sure they can see you're living in the present moment and not merely waiting for a pause in the conversation to inject some spiel you have memorized.

- *Intellectual* – you have to know your subject and yourself. When it comes to reaching the heart of another person, you have to have personal experience in the subject you're speaking about. If your audience can't feel you've lived and breathed your subject, there will be something of a credibility gap. Similarly, if you can't express what you know, that will also cause a disconnect to arise. Effective communicators are always comfortable in their own skin and confident about their own abilities. If you're not, this will come across loud and clear and get in the way of connecting.
- *Emotional* – you have to win over their hearts before you have any chance at all of winning over their minds. People are drawn to those who have charisma because there is an incredible transfer of energy going on. People will hear your words but they will feel and remember the energy and passion you bring to the subject. When you speak with people, help them feel what you feel.

Don't just give them the facts but inject your emotions and perceptions as well.

- *Verbal* – you should harness the power of the right words to maximum effect. Words are the currency of ideas and have had the power to change the world since time immemorial. Choose words which are positive and memorable. Make what you say convey the confidence you feel in graphic ways. Learn how to enlist your tone of voice, use of inflection and timing as allies in your cause.

The simple fact is you don't have to be a genius to connect with other people. Nor do you need oodles of charisma or the stage presence of a master orator. All you need do is be positive, believe in yourself, focus on others and connect with them emotionally, verbally, intellectually and visually. Everything else is just packaging that doesn't count.

> *"Any message you try to convey must contain a piece of you. You can't just deliver words. You can't merely convey information. You need to be more than just a messenger. You must be the message you want to deliver. Otherwise, you won't have credibility and you won't connect."*
>
> *– John Maxwell*

"The exact words that you use are far less important than the energy, intensity, and conviction with which you use them."

– Jules Rose, Sloans Supermarkets

"The colossal misunderstanding of our time is the assumption that insight will work with people who are unmotivated to change. Communication does not depend on syntax, or eloquence, or rhetoric, or articulation but on the emotional context in which the message is heard. People can only hear you when they are moving toward you, and they are not likely to when your words are pursuing them. Even the choicest words lose their power when they are used to overpower. Attitudes are the real figures of speech."

– Rabbi Edwin Friedman, leadership expert

"What you are speaks so loudly that I can't hear what you say."

– Ralph Waldo Emerson

"The difference between the almost right word and the right word is really a large matter-it's the difference between the lightning bug and the lightning."

– Mark Twain

"If you don't live it, it won't come out of your horn."

– Charlie Parker, jazz musician

4. CONNECTING ALWAYS REQUIRES ENERGY

Connecting with people doesn't just happen by accident. You have to be intentional about what you're doing – which means you have to put some personal energy behind what you're trying to achieve and then channel that energy strategically to succeed.

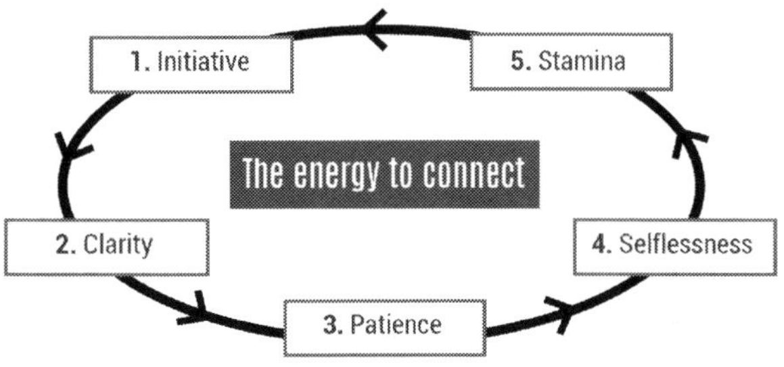

There are five proactive ways energy for connecting can and should be generated and then applied:

1. *Take the initiative and go first* – rather than waiting for the other person to try and make a connection. Do things which will break the ice and signal you want to connect. Instead of waiting for the perfect moment which may never eventuate, plunge into it.

2. *Prepare thoroughly so you can speak and act with clarity* – because people always respond to that. Know yourself and know your audience in great depth. Anticipate the key issues they care about and focus on those, Plan how you want the other person to feel at the conclusion and bring the right elements together.
3. *Be patient and slow down a little* – give time for your ideas to sink in and take root. If you're in too much of a hurry, you'll make mistakes. Go at a steady pace and tick all the right boxes rather than rushing through what you're trying to say to people.
4. *Be a giver ratherthan a taker* – meaning be selfless. Go out of your way to help other people do the things they want to do. Always have your best game on display. This will take lots of energy on your part but it's essential. People always want to connect with someone who clearly and obviously gives 100 percent at all times.
5. *Connecting requires stamina* – so recharge your batteries frequently. Build some reserves of mental, physical and emotional energy. Set up your life so you avoid activities which drain your energy but leave nothing to show. Hire people who are better than you at the stuff you're weak at. Figure out what recharges your batteries and make that a regular part of your schedule.

> *"The only thing that keeps a man going is energy and what is energy but liking life?"*
>
> – *Louis Auchincloss, novelist*

"From this day forward, I solemnly promise and declare that every time a customer comes within ten feet of me, I will smile, look him in the eye, and greet him."

– Sam Walton, founder, Wal-Mart

"The wise does at once what the fool does at last."

– Jewish proverb

5. CONNECTING IS AN ACQUIRED SKILL, NOT A TALENT

"Great communicators are not all cut from the same cloth. But they do all share the ability to connect. That does not develop by accident. You cannot expect to succeed through dumb luck. You must learn to connect with others by making the most of whatever skills and experience you have."

– John Maxwell

Why would people choose to connect with you? There are probably a handful of factors which can come into play here:

- *The relationships you enjoy* – who you know and what

your actual professional credentials are.

- *The insights you have* – what you know as a result of all the things you've been through.
- *Your track record of success* – what you've done throughout your career or in your lifetime.
- *Your abilities* – the specific set of skills and competencies you have in some specific area.
- *The sacrifices you've made thus far* – the tragedies you've overcome, the obstacles you've mastered and all the things you have endured.
- *The self confidence you possess* – and therefore the certainty you can speak with. Everyone likes being with go-getters who know what they want and where they need to head.
- *Authenticity and integrity* – the fact you walk the talk and project who you are.
- *Your advance preparation* – that you research your topic and come prepared to make a real contribution.
- *Your sense of humor* – your ability to share good jokes and have a fun time doing what you do.
- *Your ability to focus on others* – and develop solutions to their problems rather than being self-centered.
- *The fact you come across as a friend and advisor – someone others want to trust and like.*

The whole point is nobody ever has all these factors aligned right out of the box. All highly effective communicators start out as being less effective at first but then keep working at it. You will have to follow the same development trajectory for yourself. Learn how to connect and then keep on working at becoming better at this all the time. This is an area where it's the journey that counts, not the destination that's reached.

"All great speakers were bad speakers first."

– Ralph Waldo Emerson, poet and philosopher

"If you want to have better relationships, if you want to achieve personal success, or if you want to become a better leader, make connecting your goal. To do that, become a student of communication if you aren't one already. Study effective and ineffective speakers, observing what works and what doesn't. Give thought to what causes people to listen to others, and begin working on cultivating those characteristics. And wherever you go, watch how good connectors interact with people one-on-one. You can become better at connecting if you're willing to work at it."

– John Maxwell

2. FIVE PRACTICES OF WELL CONNECTED LEADERS

There are five practices anyone can do to better connect with others – regardless of your age, experience or natural ability. Learning how to do these things can significantly change your life. To become a better and more connected leader:

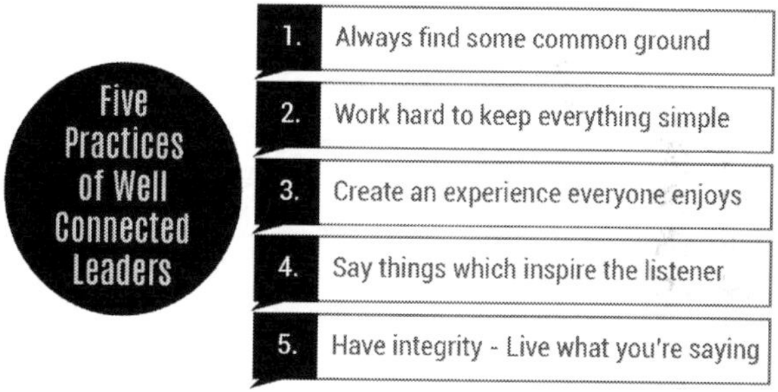

Five Practices of Well Connected Leaders

1. Always find some common ground
2. Work hard to keep everything simple
3. Create an experience everyone enjoys
4. Say things which inspire the listener
5. Have integrity - Live what you're saying

1. ALWAYS FIND SOME COMMON GROUND

"If I had to pick a first rule of communication – the practice above all others that opens the door to connection with others – it would be to look for common ground. That rule applies whether you're resolving conflict with your spouse, teaching a child, negotiating a deal, selling a product, writing a book, leading

a meeting, or communicating to an audience. It's difficult to find common ground with others when the only person you're focused on is yourself!"

– John Maxwell

This sounds so obvious you would be right to question why it is sometimes so difficult for different parties to find common ground and build on it. There are four barriers which can cause people to struggle to find common ground:

1. *Assumptions* – when you make the mistake of assuming you already know what the other party is thinking or feeling without getting around to asking them directly.
2. *Arrogance* – when you don't believe it's necessary to figure out what other people are feeling or want. You'll never really succeed in building a relationship with other people in the room if you don't care about them in the slightest.
3. *Indifference* – when you can't be bothered making an effort to figure out what others want or need.
4. *Fear of loss of control* – if you make an effort to understand what others are feeling, you may be afraid of appearing weak. Some leaders operate on the basis it's best to keep people in the dark so they won't question what's going on too rigorously.

Although some people suggest finding common ground with others is a talent, it's really a matter of cultivating the right kind of mind-set. Developing ways to find common ground is a choice. It's a skill which can be learned and acquired rather than something which is in your DNA or forget about it.

To get better at finding common ground with others, there are eight things worth doing:

1. Availability
2. Listen with empathy
3. Ask questions
4. Be thoughtful
5. Have an open mind
6. Be likeable
7. Be humble
8. Exhibit adaptability

- *Availability* – make a conscious decision to spend enough time that you get to know what's going on first-hand. Be accessible and engaged in what's going on.
- *Listen with empathy* – let others educate you about the facts of the situation. Don't be so busy talking you fail to pick up on what the other party is trying to say.
- *Ask questions* – forget what you think you know and instead be interested enough to ask some probing questions. Get beneath the surface and figure out what's going on by asking some worthwhile questions

and then waiting for an answer.

- *Be thoughtful* – go out of your way to think of others and thank them for their input.
- *Have an open mind* – and let other people come into your life. Establish common interests and build on those.
- *Be likeable* – which means care about other people and be willing to do helpful things. People always like those who like them back.
- *Be humble* – think about the needs of the other person before putting your own interests forward.
- *Exhibit adaptability* – which includes the ability to see things from another person's point of view. Move to where the other person is and see things from their perspective.

This last point in particular is critical. If you were to do nothing else other than trying to see things from the other person's perspective, your ability to connect would increase markedly. All too frequently, people see the job of a communicator as being to convey massive amounts of information to other people. A better way is to think of communication as a journey. The more you have in common with the listener, the better the chances become the other person will choose to take that journey with your help and guidance. Finding common ground opens the floodgates.

"When I'm getting ready to reason with a man, I spend one-third of my time thinking about myself and what I am going to say-and two thirds thinking about him and what he is going to say."

– Abraham Lincoln

"My greatest strength as a consultant is to be ignorant and ask a few questions."

– Peter Drucker, the "father" of modern management

"I'm curious about everything. I often ask my favorite question, 'Why?' On my television show, I probably use this word more than any other. It's the greatest question ever asked, and it always will be. And it is certainly the surest way of keeping a conversation lively and interesting."

– Larry King, broadcaster and television host

2. WORK HARD TO KEEP EVERYTHING SIMPLE

"All the great things are simple, and many can be expressed in a single word: freedom, justice, honor, duty, mercy, hope. Broadly speaking, the short words are the best, and the old words best of all."

– Winston Churchill, British prime minister and winner of the Nobel Prize for Literature

To really connect with people, don't try and impress them with your vocabulary. Instead, break everything down into simple ideas and people will invite you back again and again.

The five guidelines for keeping things simple are:

1. *Get into the habit of talking to people* – rather than trying to talk down to them. Break big ideas down into manageable chunks and then explain those chunks in simple language. Your listener will love it whenever you do that.
2. *Get to the point* – be clear, concise and quick. Great communicators think about their message in advance and stay on track when speaking. If you do the same, the odds improve that you will connect. Everyone loves clarity. When you speak, just hit the high points and let the details sort themselves out later on.
3. *Repeat your key point over and over*-and then over again. Repetition is a fundamental and undeniable law of learning. For people to pick up on and then buy in to what you say, you have to keep repeating things until they feel comfortable.
4. *Say what you want to say clearly and without ambiguity* – so everyone is on the same page. It's amazing how many misunderstandings can arise when people don't articulate their ideas well. Avoid all that by laying out your ideas in crystal clear language and logic.

Remember in the end, people will only connect to the ideas they understand so you have to be very clear and concise.

5. *Always try and say less* – and people will love you for it. Admittedly, this does sound counterintuitive but the less you say, the more people will be impressed. Replace too much information with clarity and simplicity and you'll be invited back again and again.

"Three words are essential to connect with others (1) brevity, (2) levity, and (3) repetition. Let me say that again!"

– Daniel Pink, author

"The first time you say something, it's heard. The second time, it's recognized, and the third time, it's learned."

– William Rastetter, CEO IDEC Pharmaceuticals

"Insecure managers create complexity. Frightened, nervous managers use thick, convoluted planning books and busy slides filled with everything they've known since childhood."

– Jack Welch, former CEO, General Electric

"He is one of those orators who, before he gets up, does not know what he is going to say; when he is speaking, does not know what he is saying; and when he

has sat down, doesn't know what he has said. He can compress the most words into the smallest idea of any man I've ever met."

– Winston Churchill

3. CREATE AN EXPERIENCE EVERYONE ENJOYS

If you make what you have to say interesting and enjoyable, you improve the likelihood people will connect with you. There are seven things you can try to make presentations interesting:

1. *Take responsibility for your listeners* – and focus on capturing their attention and retaining that attention throughout by doing memorable things. Great leaders don't just dump their ideas on people with a take-it-or-leave-it approach. They engage listeners and create great experiences.
2. *Communicate in your listener's world* – put your thoughts into terms they will relate to. Link what you have to say with the everyday challenges they face and your presentation will come to life because of its relevancy.
3. *Harness a great beginning* – which captures their attention from the outset. You might start with humor, pose a question or bring along a visual aid. Do something which will generate energy in the room.

4. *Activate your audience* – literally. Encourage them to take notes, to ask questions and even move about if feasible. Get people to interact with you and they will have a much better overall experience.
5. *Have one memorable phrase which will continue to resonate* – long after your presentation has ended. Martin Luther King, Jr. is still remembered today for his "I have a dream" speech. You can aspire to similar greatness. Abraham's Lincoln's Gettysburg Address was anchored around "A government of the people, by the people, for the people." Say things in interesting and original ways people will remember.
6. *Be visual* – bring your subject to life with some kind of demonstration. If that's not possible, try and use words which will stimulate the imagination of listeners. Vividness is good.
7. *Tell stories* – because these have always been the best way to capture interest and give people a good time. Embed the cold facts you need to get across in warm and engaging stories and people will love you for it. All great communicators have always used stories to good effect and you will need to do the same. People find it much easier to connect when they hear an inspiring story.

In many ways, the key to becoming a great communicator is to become the kind of person you'd love to hear in person yourself. Think about the qualities you look for in the people you connect with and then inject those same elements into what you do as a presenter.

> *"On average, prospects retain only half what we tell them. Before an hour has passed, they lose 10 percent of the little they originally knew. After sleeping on it, guess what? Another 20 percent evaporates. By the time the breakfast rush has subsided, they have avoided two near-collisions on the freeway, found notes on their desks from their bosses, and they have forgotten another 10 percent. So the entire time we have assumed a prospect has been thinking about our proposal, he or she has been forgetting about it."*
>
> *– Teri Sjodin, speaker and trainer*

> *"People have remote controls in their heads today. If you don't catch their interest, they just click you off."*
>
> *– Myrna Marofsky, management consultant*

4. SAY THINGS WHICH INSPIRES THE LISTENER

Whether you realize it or not, everyone wants to be inspired. Effective communicators connect because they inspire. This all comes down to a reasonably simple equation:

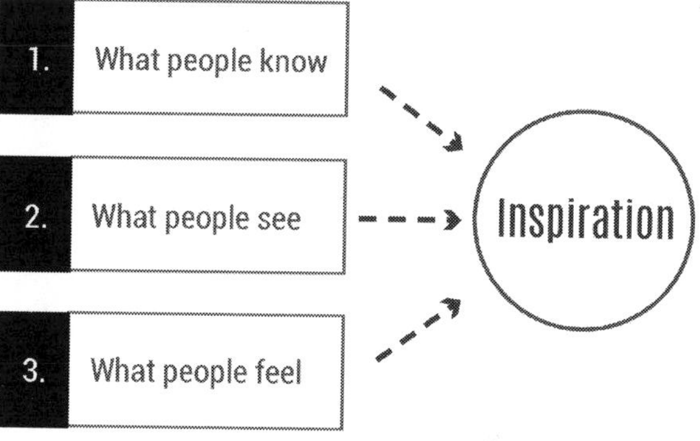

To be inspiring as a communicator, you need to bring these three different factors into play:

1. *What people know* – you have to understand your audience's feelings, desires, wishes, fears and passions. People will only trust you if they feel reassured you understand them and are focused on their needs. If you take note of what people are thinking, saying and doing and orient your presentation towards those issues, you'll connect alright. Add to what they already know to inspire.
2. *What people see* _ that you're smiling and confident about delivering something beneficial. In other words, people need to see visual signs of your conviction. They will gauge very quickly whether you believe the argument you're advancing. If you don't, you're effectively dead in the water. By contrast, if your credibility

is so strong people can practically taste it, they will sit up and take notice. The old adage states it well: "The mediocre teacher tells. The good teacher explains. The great teacher demonstrates."

3. *What people feel* – the combined impact of your passion for the subject, your self-confidence and your gratitude for them as individuals. Passion is always impressive but people want to know what the plan is for making the right things happen. They want to know what you're suggesting is worth it because you're confident about the outcome which will be achieved. They want to feel appreciated for who they are and that you have gratitude for what they bring to the table. You have to express that gratitude verbally so everyone is on the same page.

Connecting with people isn't achieved by merely entertaining them and making them feel good. You have to lead them to action based around what you're saying. Put another way, you have to say the words which will spark them into action and give them a plan for what needs to happen. Connectors provide the bridge between what people know they should be doing and what they walk out of the room committed to do tomorrow.

> *"The true purpose of inspiration isn't applause. Its value isn't in the wonder it may create or the positive feelings it may invoke in others. The true test of in-*

spiration is action. This is what makes a difference. If you desire to connect with others, you must strive to inspire people."

– *John Maxwell*

"Management is about persuading people to do things they do not want to do, while leadership is about inspiring people to do things they never thought they could."

– *Steve Jobs, CEO, Apple Computer*

5. HAVE INTEGRITY – LIVE WHAT YOU'RE SAYING

"Credibility is currency for leaders and communicators. With it, they are solvent; without it, they are bankrupt. With credibility, leaders continue to connect with people. Without it, they disconnect."

– *John Maxwell*

Your credibility as a communicator and as a leader will stand or fall on your integrity. If you have integrity, people will continue to naturally trust you. If you don't have integrity, your message will be hollow rather than bold and inspiring. The effectiveness you achieve as a communicator always relies more on the character of you as the messenger than it ever does on the character of the message itself.

To enhance your personal integrity level:

1. *Never forget you are your message* _ so the first person you have to connect with is yourself. Accept who you are and get comfortable with what you have to offer. Get comfortable in your own skin.
2. *Acknowledge your mistakes openly and candidly* – and make amends if necessary. This will boost your credibility and communicate that you value integrity highly. Thomas Jefferson once remarked: "If you have to eat crow, eat it while it's young and tender."
3. *Be accountable* – make commitments and then expect others to measure your results and judge you on what you deliver. People love that. When you keep your commitments and deliver on your promises, you create an aura of trust.
4. *Lead the way you live* – have consistency and alignment so you can say "Follow me!" and mean it. There is an undeniable leadership energy which comes from leaders who model what needs to be done in their own lives. Some great examples of this have been:
    - General Robert E. Lee who was well known for visiting his troops the night before a major battle rather than getting some sleep.
    - General George S. Patton who often went into a tight battle in the lead tank of his armor units, inspiring his troops to fight.
    - Napoleon who was frequently present on the battlefield in person when his troops went to war. One

of Napoleon's greatest protagonists, the Duke of Wellington, once commented Napoleon's presence on the battlefield was worth an extra 40,000 troops in his estimation.

5. *Tell the unvarnished truth* – no matter what the consequences. People love a straight shooter who tells it like it is. They will respect your openness and this will enhance your ability to connect out of sight.
6. *Be vulnerable* – admit your weaknesses with candor. Don't come across as someone who knows all the answers but admit you're figuring things out as you go along as well. People always form the deepest connections with those who acknowledge their weaknesses and ask for help.
7. *Follow the golden rule* – treat others the same way whether they are on the way up or the way down. Treat everyone the way you'd like to be treated regardless of their role and people will trust you and want to connect with you. This is one of those tricky things which is easy to describe but hard to do.
8. *Deliver results* – be known as someone who is credible because you've accomplished something noteworthy. Results speak with an exceptionally loud voice. Get results first and credibility will just naturally follow. Do what you're advising everyone else to do. Great communicators always speak from first-hand experience.

To be successful and to make a tangible difference in the world, you have to be a good communicator but even more you have to connect. To keep connecting over the long haul, you have to live what you're saying. Begin with yourself and make certain what you say is consistent with what you feel and what you do every day. Model what you're trying to suggest and there are no limits to what you can and will accomplish.

> *"Nothing speaks like results. If you want to build the kind of credibility that connects with people, then deliver results before you deliver a message. Get out and do what you advise others to do. Communicate from experience. To be successful in the long run, you need to do more than connect. You need to keep connecting, and you can do that only when you live what you communicate. When you do, the results can be fantastic."*
>
> *– John Maxwell*

> *"A teacher affects eternity; he can never tell where his influence stops."*
>
> *– Henry Adams*

> *"Communication always makes demands. It always demands that the recipient become somebody, do something, believe something. It always appeals to motivation."*
>
> *– Peter Drucker, management consultant*

"I always try to keep in mind this definition of success: 'Those who are closest to me and know me the best, love and respect me the most.' When the people who know how you live day in, day out, see that your words and actions align, then they can trust you, have confidence in you, and connect with you. And that makes life a great and enjoyable journey every single day."

– John Maxwell

"You cannot speak what you do not know. You cannot share that which you do not feel. You cannot translate that which you do not have. And you cannot give that which you do not possess. To give it and to share it, and for it to be effective, you first have to have it."

– Jim Rohn, author

"What can you do with the talent you have? Whatever is in you can be put to better use if you learn to connect with people. You can learn to increase your influence in every situation because connecting is more skill than natural talent. And you can learn to do it. So start taking steps. Embrace the connecting principles. Start using the connecting practices. And do something positive in your corner of the world."

– John Maxwell

Powered by Primento

The digital partner of traditional publishers

Ebook EAN: 9782806233875

Paperback EAN: 9782511042762

Made in the USA
San Bernardino, CA
31 January 2018